Dog Training

Basics of Puppy & Dog Training

by
Catherine Lewis

Contents

Introduction

This book contains proven steps and strategies on how to teach and train your dogs' basic obedience skills.

Getting a dog is a lifetime commitment. As a canine owner, you will be responsible for the health, behavior, and habits of your dog. You have to raise your pooch to become an example of man's best friend and the paradigm of its pedigree to the best of your capability.

The moment you decide to share a dog's lifetime, your journey as its teacher, parent, and buddy begins. On this trip, your house will become its house. It will become a member of your family, and it will dedicate its life to guard and adore you for the rest of its life.

You won't just be the leader of the pack; your pooch will see you like the best human. As much as your four-legged friend will do its best to please you, you must also do your best to teach it what it needs to learn as your best buddy.

Do not leave it all to chance or trial and error. If you have no idea how to raise a dog properly, chances are, you'll end up frustrated, and your buddy will feel unwanted. Make your journey together a big adventure.

This book will guide you on how to educate your puppy or dog about good manners inside and outside the house. This book has the knowledge and advice on how to raise and train your pooch obedience. This book will also guide you on how to housebreak your pup properly.

Dog Training by Catherine Lewis

Chapter 1 - The Basics

Your dog's behavior, habits, and temperament depend on you and your knowledge on dog training. The moment you choose your four-legged friend, its future begins. The clock is running fast, and there is no time to waste. The moment your puppy comes home, within the span of three months, your puppy needs to meet six primary targets to achieve its full potential.

The Six Primary Targets

Meeting these targets will determine your life together with your furry friend.

1. Your Dog Training Education

Before your search begins for your wet-nosed buddy, you must know:

- What breed of dog will suit your lifestyle

- Where to get your puppy

- When to take it home

Getting a puppy or dog should not be done on impulse, but rather an educated choice. You will be responsible for the dog's life for as long as it lives. Be wise with your decision.

Along with making the informed decision, you must also:

- Familiarize yourself with the six primary targets

- Review this book and preferably other sources too

- Observe the dog breed of your choice by searching online, there are plenty of forums and informative websites on specific breeds. You can also find information in your local library and pet store

Your life together depends on your choice and your knowledge.

2. Evaluating Your Puppy's Progress

Before you select your puppy (typically eight weeks old), you must:

- Select a good breeder

- Choose a dog that you feel a connection with

- Know how to assess a puppy's behavioral development

3. Errorless Housetraining

Before you take your new puppy home, you must ensure that on the very first day your new dog comes home you will start teaching it:

- Errorless Housetraining

- Chew toy training

What your puppy learns during the first week in its new home will set its character and habits for the years to come.

4. Socialization with People

When your puppy is 12-weeks old, it will be ready to enjoy the company of other dogs and people. By this time, it`s series of immunization is complete and it is safe to introduce and let it meet new people at home.

Ideally, your puppy must have already met many different people before you take it back home so that the pup is used to be around humans and being handled by them.

5. Bite Inhibition

By 18 weeks old, your dog's teeth and jaws can harm and hurt. It must be taught to use these weapons gently with other animals and people. It is advised that you enroll your puppy in a bite inhibition class before its 18th week.

6. Preventing Adolescent Problems

By 5-months old onwards, you must ensure that your dog learns to be:

- Well-schooled

- Well-rounded

- Remains mannerly

- Well-socialized

- Friendly

You need to ensure your dog meets unfamiliar people and dogs on a regular basis.

- Walk your puppy at least once a day

- Take it for rides in the car

- Visit your friends

You can start walking your furry friend as soon as your vet says it's safe. It will ensure that your pooch is properly socialized with other dogs and humans and able to adapt to unfamiliar noises and places. Your puppy will be less anxious when it meets something or someone new.

Chapter 2 - Choosing Your Breed

There is more than just the type or breed preference when selecting a puppy. Naturally, the dog must suit your lifestyle and personality. But there are other things to consider as well.

The "Perfect Breed"

THERE IS NO SUCH THING. If you want a marvelous furry companion, then you must properly train and socialize your pup. Regardless of the breed, a dog will grow up with a delinquent behavior when you do not raise it correctly.

Seek Guidance

Contrary to popular belief, pet store personnel, breeders, and veterinarians are not good sources of advice concerning dog behavior and training. The best training advice comes from trainers. The best dog behavior information comes from behavior counselors.

If you require more in-depth training, please visit:
www.tiny.cc/dogcoaching

If you want the hard, cold facts about puppies, go and check out a local puppy class. Talk with the owners. They will lay down the truth about life with a dog.

Keep in mind:

- Veterinarians - health advice

- Breeders - breed advice

- Pet-store personnel - product advice

Seek Several Sources and Evaluate Every Advice Carefully

When seeking help, one should apply the principle of common sense. Is it relevant? Does the information make sense? Remember that the choice of selecting a lifetime furry companion is yours. However, your choice must be an educated and well-informed one.

Regardless of the pedigree, cuteness, conformation, size, and general health, the ultimate success will entirely depend on the puppy's education regarding training and appropriate behavior.

- As long as a large dog gets regularly walked, it can live in an apartment. They bark less and settle down better.

- When trained to shush and settle down, small dogs make excellent apartment buddies.

- If the dog gets trained how to behave around children and the children are taught how to behave around dogs, any breed is good with children.

Mixed Breed or Pure Breed?

It's a personal choice. You do need to know that a pure breed dog's behavior and looks are more predictable than a mixed breed.

A mixed breed pup is one of a kind and unique. Pure breeds may potentially have a lot of health problems, and you must keep this in mind when making your choice.

You can check out the breed's basic manner, general health, and friendliness if you are visiting a pure-breed kennel by looking at the parents.

Which Breed Should You Choose?

Again, selecting the breed is a personal choice. You will eventually pick the kind you want, however, it all comes down this - research the breed-specific problems and qualities, and then investigate the best way to raise and teach your pup. The success or the failure of your puppy's temperament and behavior is in your hands. Here is how you do it.

1. Find at least six owners of the dog breed you want.

2. Talk to the owners about the dog's bad points

3. Meet the adult dogs themselves; work and play with them.

You will get an idea of what you are getting yourself into by observing the adult dogs of the breed you want. Try to answer the following questions.

1. Do the dogs allow strangers to pet them?

2. Do they sit?

3. Do they walk well on a leash?

4. Are they collected? Calm?

5. Are they rambunctious? Hyperactive?

6. Do the dogs allow you to examine their eyes and ears?

7. Do the dogs allow you to open the muzzle?

8. Can you make them roll over on their back?

9. Are the owner's gardens and houses in good condition?

10. Do the dogs like other dogs and people?

Dog Breed and Temperament

Although there may be considerable variation regarding behavior, personality and temperament, adequately trained and socialized dogs will have better temperaments than dogs that are uneducated.

Genetic or hereditary factors also play a role in the dog's personality and behavior. Still, your dog's desired sedentary behavior is wholly dependent on how you raise it.

To give you a clear picture, your dog bites, barks, wags its tail, and marks its territory with urine generally for genetic reasons. However, the danger of its bite, the location of its urine marks, and the eagerness of its tail wag will largely depend on the way you train and socialize your pup.

Chapter 3 - Right Time to Get a Pup

Certainly not before you are ready, the right time is after you have finished your dog training education and of course, when the puppy is ready.

Leaving Home Can Be Traumatic for Puppies

If the pup leaves its original home too early, it will miss the opportunity for its pup-mother and pup-pup interactions. When this happens, the puppy may grow up under-socialized towards its kind. On the other hand, if it stays too long in its original home, it will become attached to its family, and it will be a harder transition when it leaves. A late shift also delays the critical socialization of the pup to its new family.

Eight Weeks Old is the Right Age

An eight-week-old pup is old enough to safely meet and play with other dogs in parks and puppy classes. It is still old enough to form strong bonds with the members of its new family.

However, it is vital to consider the level of dog expertise in the pup's new home. The furry creature may be better leaving earlier or staying longer. First-time dog owners are advised to consider an older, well-trained, socially mature pup. A diligent breeder is often more qualified to housetrain, socialize, and chew toy train a pup. But when the breeder is not an expert, it is better to move the puppy to its new home.

Choose a Good Breeder

It is similarly important to consider the expertise of the breeder. A good breeder will:

- Rank a pup's physical health and mental well-being above looks

- Keep well-trained and people friendly adult dogs

- Initially, educate your prospective puppy to be well-trained and well-socialized

- Take time to see the way you get along with the older dogs before they let you meet the pups

- Supervise you with a pup when you don't know how to handle an adult dog

- Raise dog's indoors, around human companionship and influence

- Carefully choose a prospective puppy owner

When the parents of your prospective pup are friendly, it is proof of proper training and socialization from the breeder.

Puppy vs. Adult

Of course, there are positively several advantages of raising a dog from a pup. If you know how to train it, then you can mold your companion's temperament and behavior to suit you and your lifestyle.

When you have a doubt about your training capability, then an adolescent dog with an obedience title or one who passed one or more obedience tests is a more suitable friend.

When the dog is two years old, its manners, habits and temperament are, for better or for worst, well established. However, traits and habits may alter over time, though not as flexible as that of a young dog.

Nevertheless, you can always consider rescue centers or shelter dogs and choose the one with the personality you like. Adopting from a rescue organization or shelter can be an excellent alternative. Some of these canines are well- behaved, needing only a home. Others have few character problems and only require remedial education.

A dog from an animal shelter or a rescue center is also a good choice for people who work and those who do not have the time to raise and train a puppy.

Otherwise, if set on raising your pup, educate yourself properly about dog training.

Please do not add to the number of shelter and rescued dogs by being an irresponsible canine owner.

Temperamental and behavioral problems in dogs, even the most common ones, are easily preventable with the proper training. Annoying habits often happen when an owner does not know how to educate a dog properly.

Shopping List: Things You Need Before Getting a Puppy/Dog

Getting a puppy or a dog is similar to rearing children. Your four-legged best friend will need the following essentials. You must have these essential items ready before you take your furry buddy home.

- Leash
- Collar
- Chew toy
- Water bowl
- Food bowl
- Cleaning agents
- A playpen, x-pen or a baby gate

Chapter 4 - Housebreaking a Pup

Housebreaking is a term that just means toilet etiquette for puppies. Training your furry buddy the proper way to relieve itself is the very first step of training and adjustment to its new home.

Inside, Outside or Both?

It's the most important question, which you need to answer even before you take your furry buddy home. Do you want to toilet train it inside or outside? Or do you wish to mix both? It depends on your personal preference and your living situation. There is no wrong or right way.

Indoor Potty Training

Obviously, if you live in a building without easy access to the street or a yard, then this is the appropriate potty training for your dog since short and repeated trips outsides will virtually be impossible.

Set aside space in your house as an exclusive space for toilet use. Be sure that the area is away from your pooches water and food.

Please note that indoor training is best suited for dogs of a smaller breed. If you are planning to get a large breed, like a Labrador, indoor potty training is impractical.

Also, be reminded that if you indoor train your pup; you may have to frequently deep clean to remove stains and smells of accidents.

Outdoor Potty Training

If you have access to a yard or a quiet street, then you owe it to your home, dog and yourself to do the training outdoors.

Evidently, potty training outdoors is easier and cleaner since once your four-legged buddy gets trained, there is less chance of mess on the floors and carpets in your house.

On the other hand, you will need to brave the weather of the outdoors - rain, sleet, or snow, scoop your pooch's poop, and properly discard it.

Mixed Potty Training

If you like to take your dog out when you have the time to spend with it, then you can teach it both. However, it can be confusing for your dog, and they might not get it immediately, which can lead to potty problems. Nevertheless, if you do it with proper planning and care, you will be able to teach this to your dog successfully.

Housebreaking Methods

Housebreaking can be difficult or easy depending on the method you choose. The most modern, common, humane, and successful approaches are the following. We will discuss each method in the following chapters. For now, here are the basics of each technique and what to expect when you are housebreaking a puppy.

Crate Training

Using a crate are the vital elements of this method. This Method is efficient, fast, and allows you to work with your pup's natural instincts. The dog will see the crate as its den, and dogs always keep their space clean of urine and feces.

Paper Training

The idea of this method is to teach your pup to relieve on papers or a pad inside the house. Once the puppy is consistent, you will begin to move the paper or pads closer to the door, and then finally outside. Once your puppy learns to do its business outside, you can remove the papers or the pad, unless, you are toilet training indoors of course.

Constant Supervision

This approach is just what it says it is, constantly supervising your furry friend. You must be ready to respond, to take the pup outside when it shows signs of relieving itself.

The upside is that this is the cheapest method since it will only need your constant attention. The downside, you must certainly not allow any accident to happen inside the house, or you will suffer a setback in your training. This approach also needs more concentration, effort, and is time-consuming.

Umbilical Cord Training

This method combines constant supervision and requires you to attach your pup to your body using a leash. This technique will enable you to always supervise your puppy as you attach it to yourself.

Potty Training Length

It will vary from puppy to puppy. However, you can expect the following:

- Very young pups have little control of their bladder and bowel

- Smaller breeds, including Toy breeds, can take as long as 16 weeks.

- Larger breeds have better control of theirs.

- Some pups learn faster than others.

- Some will learn within days, and some take a couple of weeks to learn.

- Frequent toilet trips are necessary since even if they have come to control their bowels and bladder, a pup cannot hold for long.

- A puppy may learn and then forget. It is entirely reasonable. Continue potty training and it will eventually remember what to do.

- A 16 –week old a puppy can learn proper potty habits, with a few accidents here and there.

- With proper housebreaking, you can expect your puppy to be fully potty trained by 6-7 months old.

Puppy Bowel and Bladder Control

Just to give you a general idea, a 2-month old puppy can hold its bladder for about 30-45 minute. For a three month old pup, 1 1/2 – 2 hours is the maximum. At four months old, the puppy can hold it for an hour, five months for 2 hours, six months for 3 hours, and so on.

Toilet Time at Night

If you do not give water or feed to your pooch 2 hours before sleep time, take your dog out to relieve, and then it will not have to potty at night.

An 8-week old puppy will ideally last 4-5 hours. It will vary from pup to pup, of course, which means your pup may have to potty at least once at night.

Do the following tips:

- Set a timer for alarm 4 hours after bedtime.

- Get up. Let your pup out, whether it is making a sound or not. It will most likely be noisy to inform you that it needs to go.

The time your pup can last will lengthen with each passing week. When it is 16 weeks old, your furry friend will last 7 hours, and you won't even have to get up in the middle of the night for a potty session. If you are lucky, it may reach the 7-hour max between 10-16 weeks old.

Potty Schedule

It depends on when your pup last drank and ate. Its activities and preference are also factors. However, most puppies need to go shortly after drinking or eating.

The general rule is to take your pup to its bathroom spot

- As soon as you rise from bed, first thing in the morning

- Before the last awake person goes to bed

- Immediately after your puppy wakes up from a nap during the day

- Within 30 minutes after eating

- Within 15 minutes after drinking

- After play or any excitement, such as meeting a new person

You will also need to take it to its bathroom spot approximately at the time mentioned below depending on their age.

Age	Bathroom Schedule (every)
8 weeks	30 minutes
10 weeks	45 minutes
3 months	1 – 1 1/2 hours
4 months	2 hours or so
5 months	3 hours

Again, this will vary from pup to pup.

Potty Accidents

It is always advised to bring your puppy to the veterinarian before you start housebreaking. Accidents during the training process could be due to health reasons and not bad behavior. Urinary tract infection, gastroenteritis, and medical problems that affect the genitalia or internal organ can cause frequent potty sessions than normal.

Chapter 5 - Crate Training

Dogs are naturally den dwellers. In fact, dogs feel secure and safe in small, enclosed spaces. The crate is a perfect den place for them. Especially when used correctly and adequately, it is far from being cruel and offers many benefits to both dog owner and the pup.

- Speeds up learning during housebreaking

- Keeps the puppy safe during travel and at home

- Gives your pup a place of its own

- Provides a place for your dog when it needs quiet time

- Prevents the formation of bad habits

- Safeguards your belongings

Please remember that this technique is a combination of confinement and supervision, NOT DEFINITE CONFINEMENT.

Using Your Puppy's Natural Instincts

As mentioned earlier, dogs instinctively tend to keep their den clean since they associate it as their sleeping and resting place. Virtually, crate training is teaching your pup that the crate is its den, which taps in to your furry buddy's natural instinct to keep it clean.

There are also quite a few benefits using crate training. Please, always keep in mind your puppy's bladder and bowel control.

Provides More Opportunity for Praise

When you are TEMPORARILY busy, you can keep your pup inside the crate for a SHORT-PERIOD. The moment you take it out, immediately grab your puppy to its designated bathroom spot, it will be ready to go.

It provides you more chances to reward and praise it for a proper toilet habit.

Prevents Pooping in the Wrong Places

The majority of poop and pee accidents occur when you are distracted and unable to watch and catch your pup when it is showing signs of wanting to go.

If you place your pup in a crate, it will try to hold it and wait for release time. Please remember that you must correctly apply supervision techniques during this process.

Teaches Bowel and Bladder Control

When a pup is very young, it will just leak. The puppy can't help it, and it won't know it`s coming since it has no body control during this period.

As the pup grows, it will be able to hold it for short periods, but because it has uncontrollable leaking, it eventually poops and pees no matter of when and where.

When you teach your pup that the crate is its den, it will try to hold it in to keep its place clean. Your puppy will learn that it does not have to go right away and keep it.

When you teach your pup this method correctly, it can speed up the housebreaking.

Preparing the Crate

You should not place any water or food inside the crate because if your pup drinks and eats, the need to eliminate will follow.

Where and how small or large the container should be for your pup should also be considered.

The Size of Your Pup's Crate

It should not be too large since this may allow your puppy to use one part as the sleeping area and the other area as a toilet. It should be just large enough to allow your pup to lie on its side

28

with the legs comfortably stretched out so that it can quickly turn around and stand up straight. The crate should not be cramped.

Crate Location

Place your pup's crate in the room where your family spends most of your time together, like the kitchen or the living room. You can even move and transfer the crate to any room in the house where you and your family will spend time together.

Never use the crate as a punishment.

Do not place the crate away from the places where you usually stay. If you do this, it will make your furry buddy feel isolated and unwanted. Dogs always want to be close with their pack. Since you are now its family, it now belongs to your pack.

Introducing the Crate to Your Pup

It is important that your new friend thinks of the crate as its comfort zone. The crate must be its place of enjoyment and security.

1. Occasionally put small pieces of dog biscuits or kibble in the crate throughout the day. The edible treasures will reinforce a positive association. You should also feed it in the crate. If your pup hesitates, you can start by feeding your puppy in front of it, then just right inside the doorway, and finally inside the crate.

2. Pet and praise your pup when it enters the crate. You should not force the puppy into it by pushing or pulling. It is important that at this stage you only use inventive methods. Lure your pup into it using a treat, and then give another treat once it has successfully entered. Leave the door open. Repeat this process several times a day.

   You can make it an enjoyable and educational game.

   • Drop a small dog biscuit in the crate without alerting your pup.

- Call to it and ask, "Where is the treat?" while directing the dog to the crate and using an encouraging and friendly voice.

- Praise the pup lavishly when it discovers the treat. The treat is automatically the reward.

- Allow your puppy to leave the crate freely all times during the game.

- You can later substitute the treat with a toy or a ball.

Training with the Crate

1. Make sure that your pup has recently relieved before putting your puppy in the crate.

2. Immediately carry your puppy to its bathroom spot when you take it out of the crate. Carrying it is important for young pups as they tend to let it go as soon as they feel the floor outside their crate. They won't if they are being carried. Don't forget to lavishly praise your pup when it goes.

Scheduling Your Pup's Crate and Toilet Timing

You must crate your puppy around its regular toilet time.

Feed your puppy on a regular schedule to predict when it needs to eliminate. Once you have tracked your pup's toilet pattern you can easily know when to take it to the designated bathroom spot.

Crate Your Pup before Its Toilet Time

Depending on your pup's size and age, you can put it in the crate 15-20 minutes before your pup's routine bathroom time. Your puppy will usually be ready to go on schedule.

If your dog does not go, return your puppy to the crate for 5-15 minutes, and then try again. Repeat this process until it eliminates. Don't forget to praise your pup when it does a good job.

- Do not leave your puppy in the bathroom area. It must have positive reinforcement for a good job.

- Be patient. It will take time for your pup to understand what you are teaching it. If you bring your puppy back inside the house too soon, it may make an accident.

- Do not give your puppy too many treats. This can foul its digestive system and your ability to calculate the potty break.

- Do not scream, throw things, or yell at your pup if you see that it starts to go. The best way is to startle it by making a loud sound or clapping. Immediately carry your puppy to the designated bathroom spot. Wait until it goes.

You can enjoy a supervised playtime after your pup has done its business.

What to Do When You Are Busy

The key to crate training is supervision. If you can't give your pup undivided attention for any reason, such as when you are on the phone or taking a bath, you must briefly put your puppy in the crate.

If you get too preoccupied, your pup may sneak off to empty in an undesignated bathroom spot, or worse, your puppy will eliminate where it stands. This can set back your training.

Barking Inside the Crate

If your pup cries incessantly inside its crate, it could be that your dog is suffering from separation anxiety, anxious about being alone, or crated too soon.

Do not take your pup out of the crate if it cries or barks, this will teach your puppy to make more noise if it wants to go out to eliminate.

Your dog may just need more exercise, or you may not have given your pup enough attention. Increase your play time or the amount of exercise.

When Pup Poops in the Crate

It is rare for a puppy to do its business in the crate whilst being crated, at the right age or put in a crate of the right size. However, if you notice that your pup is doing so, it could be that:

- Your buddy is too young to have control of its bowel or bladder

- You are giving your pup a wealthy or poor diet, or large meals

- You forgot to make it to the toilet before crating

- Your pup may have worms, loose or gaseous stools, drank copious amounts of water, is suffering an illness, or experiencing severe separation anxiety.

When NEVER to Use a Crate

- Never crate your puppy longer than it can hold its bowel or bladder. If you leave your pup for too long, it will potty inside the crate, which can hurt your training.

- Never crate your puppy if it has a history of relieving in a crate. Some pups, adopted and rescued, in particular, have picked up bad toilet habits in their former life. You will need to teach your puppy not to eliminate in the home before crating.

- Never crate your pup if it is ill. Remember that you must associate the crate as its den.

Is Crate Training for You?

Crate training is recommended and suitable for anyone. But it's important to have a backup plan when you can't be at home.

Even if you have full-time to supervise your new buddy, you will need to use, to a degree, additional training techniques. You can use a mix of crating and constant supervision when you are at home as much as you possibly can

When you are not at home, incorporating the crate and paper training, you can confine your puppy to an area of the house, such as the kitchen.

Place your pup's crate at one end of the kitchen and papers on the other end for a toilet. Seal the kitchen.

In rare circumstances, some puppies, mainly rescued and adopted ones have a phobia with crates. You should choose a different training method.

Chapter 6 - Paper Training

Traditionally, the idea of this training is to teach a pup to do its business on old newspaper in a designated bathroom area, making it easier to clean up since the paper holds and absorbs the feces and urine.

Nowadays, litter trays, puppy pads, sod boxes, and even fake grass are used, but the approach remains the same.

Equipment

- Old newspapers

- Food treats

- Cleaning agents

- Playpen, x-pen, or baby gates, depending on where you will confine your fur baby when you are not home

Other options:

- Puppy pads – unscented or scented absorbent pads that to encourage a pup to eliminate.

- Litter boxes - similar to what a cat uses,

The Method

This approach relies on the facts that pups:

- Learn to relieve themselves in the same place where they have regularly been before

- Want to go where they can smell that they have been before

- Prefer to eliminate on soft and covered surfaces rather than cold, hard floors

You will cover a relatively wide area with paper, slowly reducing the area covered with paper, and slowly moving the paper to the bathroom.

Six Easy Steps to Paper Training:

1. Decide on your pup's bathroom spot.

- A smaller area where you can confine your furry buddy with a playpen, x-pen, or baby gate.

- Opt for tiled, hardwood, or linoleum floor for easy cleaning in case of accidents.

- Avoid a carpeted area since pups prefer the softness and may do their business on the carpet and not the paper.

- The laundry room, kitchen or bathroom is ideal

- If you are using a playpen or x-pen, you can place a plastic tarpaulin before placing the paper to protect the floor and for easier cleaning.

2. Cover the whole area or room with newspaper.

It will teach your pup that it must and can do its business on paper.

- At one end of the area or room, set up your pup's bed, its water bowl, and place a few toys.

- Bring your furry friend into the area.

3. Clean up after your pup as soon as you can.

- Do not leave the dirty paper too long. You need to teach and get your puppy used to a clean place.

- Keep a piece of the soiled paper. Use it to encourage your pup to relieve in the spot you want

- Thoroughly clean the area of odors and stains. It is important so your dog won't eliminate in this place once you start removing the papers.

- Place the soiled paper you kept at one end of the area, away from your pup's water and bed. Cover it with a fresh layer of paper. Since pup's like to go where they can smell their spot, this will encourage it to relieve there.

Cut down the covered area into a spot.

You will notice that a few days later, your pup will do its business in that particular one area.

- Start by removing 1/3 of the paper under your pup's water and bed.

- Watch your puppy carefully. If its starts to relieve in an uncovered area, immediately intervene and direct your puppy to the paper. Praise your puppy as it does its business.

- Praise your pup any time it eliminates on paper without you helping out.

4. Reduce the area covered with paper.

Once your dog is regularly relieving on paper, begin to lessen the paper-covered area.

- Start with your pup's bed area, removing the paper, leaving the paper only in the farthest area away from it.

- If you observe your dog doing its business outside the designated area, you may have to increase the covered area once more.

5. Move the papers to the final bathroom spot.

Once the paper has reduced to a couple of sheets, you can start moving the paper to the designated toilet area. It can be inside or outside.

If your dog makes a mistake off paper, go back a couple of steps by adding paper and progress slowly. Clean the area thoroughly since it could be that there is odor left in that spot.

- Inside Bathroom – keep the paper in the chosen toilet spot.

- Outside – move the paper along a wall, day by day, relocating it towards the exit.

    At the same time, place some paper outside and encourage your pup to do its business there. When the paper is right beside the exit, watch your puppy closely. When it begins to potty on the paper inside, take your pup outside to use the paper there.

    Once your puppy learns to go outside, completely remove the paper indoor. Your furry friend will eventually want to go outside to do its business.

    Watch your buddy carefully for a couple of days to make sure it is doing it outside.

Disadvantages

Although paper training is easier compared to other training methods since it takes less effort and supervision, there are drawbacks.

- This technique teaches your pup that it is alright to do its business inside. It's fine if you are planning on a permanent toilet indoors. But if you intend on toilet outdoors, this will confuse your pup, and it may take longer for you to housebreak it.

- You will have more accidents, up until your puppy is old enough.

- Your puppy may become so good with the paper that it may do its business on paper lying around.

- You will need to clean dirty papers many times a day since you have to remove traces of odor immediately, compared to other techniques where you take the pup outside or a designated spot to eliminate.

- Your puppy may think that it can only eliminate on paper, which can be a problem when there is no paper on your walks or yard. To avoid this, always encourage your fur buddy to do its business outside by lavishly praising it when it does.

Is Paper Training for You?

These methods are best for people who are regularly not at home for many hours, individuals who have a mobility problem, and those who live in high buildings.

If you are using another method of housebreaking, you can use this approach as a backup plan when you are not around.

Chapter 7 - Constant Supervision

This technique means what it says - One hundred percent, all of the time, constant supervision. I cannot be more redundant than this. You must watch your pup with eyes like a hawk to ensure that it does not go potty on the carpets and floors.

The constant supervision house training covers a range of techniques that don't involve the use of a crate. Instead, it relies on always watching your dog or puppy, 100% of the time.

The Basic Technique:
1. Never leave your pup alone or unwatched.

It only takes seconds for a young fur baby to relieve itself. You must pay close attention to prevent this.

2. Watch for your pup's toilet behavior or signal.

The moment your puppy shows signs of pooping, you must immediately take your dog to the bathroom spot. Signs can include:

- Ground sniffing
- Squatting
- Circling around
- Going to a quiet spot

3. Direct your pup to the right spot.

Sound like a lot of work? You can make things easier by:

- Have your puppy sleep beside you or sit in your lap. Pups will generally not do it on you. However, some do make that mistake, peeing especially.

- Use the umbilical method. Attach your dog to you using a leash and walk around the house with it in tow.

What You Need and How to Prepare

The basic equipment includes:

- Leash

- Collar

- Food treats for reward

- Cleaning equipment for accidents

- During the time when you have to go out of the house, you will need a playpen or a baby gate

Confinement is Necessary

You can't always supervise your pup. If you do not have a crate, and you need to go out, you can confine it in a large but pup-proofed area of the house. You can:

- Use a pet barrier or a baby gate to restrict it to a room, usually the kitchen or a bathroom.

- Use an x-pen or playpen to keep your pup out of trouble.

Be sure that the space is large enough to place water and bed on one end and at one end some puppy pads or paper for a toilet.

Is Constant Supervision for You?

This approach is best for people who can spend all day with their pup, those who do not want to use the crate, and those who have adopted a rescue or shelter a dog with crate phobia.

Drawbacks

- Constant supervision without breaks can be tiring.

- Difficult to do since life gets in the way, such as cooking, washing, household chores, phone calls, visitors, and more.

- When you make a slip, your pup can sneak off and make a mistake.

- More accidents and mess. There is no pad or paper when your pup does its business when you are unable to watch it.

Recommendation

Utilize paper training and playpen or baby gate when you cannot supervise your puppy.

Chapter 8 - Umbilical Cord Training

This technique is based on constant supervision; your pup will be attached to you all the time by a leash. It is going to ensure that you will be able to interrupt, immediately correct and redirect your dog to the right spot when it is showing signs of needing to go.

Equipment

You will need the following:

- Leash – 6-foot length is recommended to give your pup freedom to move about while being close enough to you.

- Food treats

- Cleaning agents for accidents

You will also need:

- Exercise pen or baby gate to confine your pup when you have to leave it alone.

Training Guide

The basic steps are:

1. Get your pup used to wearing a collar and leash.

   This may take some time. Some pups immediately get used to the collar and leash, but some are adverse to them.

2. Attach your pup to you or a family member.

   - Loop the leash through your belt or around your wrist. It's not recommended to loop the leash around your ankle because your pup will grow stronger and it will be able to pull you over.

   - Go about your business as usual, with your pup following you around of course.

- If you are watching a TV or settling down for a while, you can attach the leash to a sturdy item or furniture near you.

3. Take your pup to the bathroom.

On the regular schedule that is appropriate for your pup's age, take it to the bathroom spot.

- Watching for signs that your pup is about to do its business, such as whining, squatting, agitated circling, ground sniffing or trying to get away from you.

- Reward and praise your puppy lavishly.

4. Correct your pup.

If you catch your fur buddy about to do its business in an inappropriate area, do not get angry or shout. Calmly but firmly tell it, "No". Lead your pup to the right place.

5. Watch carefully and use intervals for outdoor training.

When you take your pup for its spot for a scheduled poop time, or if your dog shows signs of eliminating but it does not go, take the puppy back inside the house (if training outside) or go back doing your usual chores.

Depending on your pup's age, in 5, 10, or 20 minutes, take it to the spot for another try.

Be vigilant because puppies usually go soon after interruption or after an attempt to go.

6. Release your pup for a short time.

Depending on your pup's age, you can give them freedom off the leash. However, this is a supervised free time, meaning you are close by to watch it.

- Under 12 weeks – 3-5 minutes

- 12-16 weeks - 10 minutes

- Over 16 weeks – 15 minutes

Increase your pup's freedom time as it gets older. Over time, your dog can be trusted off leash.

Some Confinement Is Necessary

Like all training methods, you will need to confine your pup when you become preoccupied. Use the paper method as a supplementary approach. The pen or a small room will serve your pups confinement at night.

Disadvantages

This training builds a strong bond between you and your fur baby. However, the drawback of this approach is having your dog attached to you all the time, which can be tiring.

If you have chosen to use this method, you can use it together with crate training to get most of the benefits of the two approaches. Another option is to use it jointly with an exercise pen or papered room.

Is Umbilical Cord Training for You?

Like constant supervision, this method is best for people who work at home or have time on their hands. However, you can use this method together with other methods.

This technique is not suitable for large dogs.

Recommendations

- Do not leave your puppy unsupervised. A 2-3 minute without supervision can end up in accidents.

- Do not let your pup wander with its leash dragging behind because it can snag on things.

- A collar and leash are choking hazards. If you are not on the other end or unable to watch your pup very carefully, the leash must come off.

- Use a breakaway, quick release collar as a safety precaution.

- If you must tether your dog to something, be sure it's something secure and heavy, one that will not topple or fall on your pup.

- Every family member is suggested to take turns and take part. It will not only bond the pup to the whole family, but it will also divide time to cover the hours of the day.

Chapter 9 - Your Pup's Diet

The quality of food you give to your pooch will affect how often and how much it needs to go to the toilet and influence your housebreaking.

If you want to learn how to make your own dog food which is the more healthy choice, please visit **www.tiny.cc/healthydogfood**

Always Give Your Dog High-Quality Dog Food

Low-quality foods are indeed cheap, but these kinds contain filler ingredients that may be hard to digest for your pup. Plus, they provide less nutritional value.

On the other hand, high-quality foods contain a higher nutritional value with little cheap fillers. These foods get digested slower, and your pup will be able to extract the nutrients better, which makes its stool firmer and therefore easier to hold in.

Your buddy will learn bowel control faster, which is to prefer when housebreaking.

Choosing the Right Food

Finding the right food that is suitable for your furry friend can be a task but it is an important one.

Find Good Food and Stick to It

If you suddenly change your pup's diet, it could likely lead to an upset stomach or diarrhea.

When You Need To Change Your Pup's Food

Do this slowly if you must.

- Mix in some of the new brand into the old.

- Increase the ratio 10% per day.

- The switch should be completed in 10 days.

Follow the recommended ratio below:

Day	Old Brand	New Brand
1	90 %	10 %
2	80 %	20 %
3	70 %	30 %
4	60 %	40 %
5	50 %	50 %
6	40 %	60 %
7	30 %	70 %
8	20 %	80 %
9	10 %	90 %
10	------	100 &

Feed on Schedule

Dogs are certainly creatures of habit. If you feed, train, exercise and potty your pup the same time every day, it will adapt and learn this schedule. Feeding your pup same time every day means it will do its business on schedule every day, as well. Your puppy will learn to expect when toilet time is coming.

Avoid Free Feeding Like the Plague

If your puppy eats at random times, then you cannot expect, or rather, not predict when the poop is coming.

- Feed your pup 3-4 meals the same time every day. Leave the food for 15 minutes, and then remove it until it's time for the next meal.

Water and Pee

How much and how often your pup drinks determines how much and how often it needs to pee.

Your Pups Water Access

It is not advised to limit your pup's access to water. It must be able to drink whenever it needs too.

Some fur babies do drink too much, which makes housebreaking harder. Some drink a lot for no particular reason, but there can be a medical reason for this.

How Much Water a Pup Needs

This will depend on:

- Breed

- Diet

- Size

- Age

- Level of activity

- Medical advice

Provide your pup constant water access and monitor how much it drinks. Most pups will regulate their drink to a time when they are thirsty.

Remember that after play or exercise and during hot weather, your pup's need for water will increase.

Checking for Dehydration

There are two ways to do this.

1. Pinch your dog's neck, stretch the skin up, outwards and then let go. If it snaps back quickly to position, then it is getting enough water. If it eases back gently and becomes wrinkled, then your dog is dehydrated.

2. Run your finger over your pup's gum. It should be very wet. If it is sticky or worse, it is dry, your dog is dehydrated.

Checking for Over-Hydration

Excessive drinking can cause lethargy. It can also be a sign that it's liver or kidney problem or it could be signs of diabetes. If your pup starts drinking excessively that cannot be explained by exercise or warm weather, then something could be wrong.

Restrict Water Access 2 Hours before Bed

For the apparent reason - you do not want to take your pup out many times at night. Bring them to potty before bedtime.

Chapter 10 - Basic Obedience Training

Training your pup obedience is important in the development of its behavior. You can start training it to follow basic commands at any age. It's better to start sooner.

What You Need:

1. A Place to Practice

This area should be free from distractions when you are just beginning to teach your pup. As it learns the commands, you can later move to an area with distractions to improve your dog's focus.

2. Rewards

It can be toys or treats. Find out which is best for your dog. If you are using treats, make sure that these are small to avoid giving your pup too much food.

3. Collar and Leash

Use size and age appropriate collar for your puppy. The ideal leash length is six feet.

4. Realistic Expectations

It may take some time for your puppy to understand what you mean, so be patient. Make each session short, about 15 minutes. When you are struggling with a command, move to another. Come back to the ones you are struggling with later on.

Basic Commands

These are the most useful commands you can teach your dog.

Sit

1. Have your dog stand in front of you.

2. Get your dogs attention by showing it a treat in your hand.

3. Slowly move the hand with the treat up and over your dogs head.

4. Slowly guide your dog into a sitting position by moving your hand over its head towards its tail.

5. As your pup moves into the position, give the command "sit".

6. As soon as it sits, give the treat to your dog and praise it for a job well done.

Down

1. Lead your dog into the sit position.

2. Show it the treat in your hand.

3. Hold the treat in front of your dog's nose.

4. Guide your dog by slowly moving the hand with the treat towards the ground, giving the command "down". If the dog slouches in the process, move your hand away to guide it further.

5. As soon as your dog's in the right position, give it the treat and praise.

Stay

1. Tell your dog to "sit" or lay "down".

2. Stand in front of your dog, holding your hand up, palms open in a stop gesture while saying "stay".

3. Keep eye contact with your dog and take a step back. Continue saying "stay".

4. If the dog stays in position, move back and give it the reward.

5. If your dog breaks position, guide it back to "sit" or "down".

Come

1. Tell your dog to "sit" or lay "down".

2. Make the dog "stay".

3. Walk a few steps away.

4. Gesture your hand in a come motion while saying "come". You should only have to say the command "come" once.

5. As soon as the dog reaches you, reward and praise it.

6. Once your dog improves, you can start training it without the leash in a safe and fenced area. If it does not follow the command, use a long lead until it can follow the command correctly.

Chapter 11 - Eliminate Bad Behaviors

It does not matter how much we love our furry buddies; nature can always get the best of them. It is essential that we train them to curb their unsightly behavior and teach them good canine manners.

Digging

Dogs like to dig and they will when they have the opportunity.

Don't Leave Your Buddy Outside

Without supervision, your dog is going to find ways to entertain itself. It means digging all over the yard. Only allow your buddy to go outside when you are there watching it.

Playtime and Exercise

Boredom will strike when your pooch doesn't get adequate activities. Burn off your dog's energy by:

- Taking it for a long walk
- Playing games, such as tug-of-war or fetch
- Doing several training sessions daily
- Taking it to a dog park
- Getting it involved in dog sports

Don't Allow Toys Outside

Dogs, by nature, are compelled to bury their possessions. Only bring toys if you're going to engage them with your pooch and if you are there to supervise.

Give Your Buddy a Spot for Digging

Buy your pooch a sandbox. Bury your dog's favorite toys in it and watch it have fun digging them out. You can also assign an area in your yard as a digging spot. If your dog digs outside the area, tell it "no" and then redirect to the correct place. Don't forget to praise your dog when it is digging in the right area.

Enroll Your Pooch in a Dog Sport

Dog sports will provide your pooch an outlet for its natural inclination to dig. It's also an excellent way to burn off mental and physical energy.

Watch the Temperature

Dogs will dig a hole in a cold spot when the weather is warm. During warmer days, be sure to provide it with a shady area in the yard and don't leave your dog outside for extended periods.

Chewing

Dogs chew when they are teething, are bored, have excess energy, is anxious or when they are curious (especially puppies).

Provide Your Pooch with Plenty of Chew Toys

When you catch your dog chewing things it shouldn't, quickly correct the behavior by making a sharp noise. Immediately replace such items with a chew toy. Don't forget to give your dog sufficient playtime and exercise to burn off energy and boredom.

Begging

This behavior is a bad habit, which unfortunately, most dog parents tolerate or encourage.

Never Give Food at the Table

Your pooch won't learn to beg if you don't teach it in the first place. You can teach your dog to go to its spot while you eat or take it to another room. If your dog behaves, then give it a treat only after you finished eating.

Not Coming When Called

We all know this behavior. Your dog pretends to be deaf when clearly, it heard you calling.

Always Praise When Your Dog Comes

In this manner, your dog will learn that it's good to come to you.

Don't Chase

When you pooch doesn't come, call for it while moving away. If your dog still doesn't come, tell it to sit and go to it.

Run Away

Running away from your dog may make it come after you.

Say "Here" or "Come."

Your dog may not understand that you want it to come when you call its name. If you know how to whistle, train your dog to come to you when you whistle. Don't forget to praise and reward.

Pulling on the Leash

Never allow your dog to pull. Make sure your dog walks calmly beside you or it will learn that pulling pays off.

Keep the Leash Short but Loose

Don't give your dog too far a slack so that it can wander off far from you. Your dog will learn that there is an acceptable distance when you are walking it with a leash.

Stop When Your Dog Pulls

Whenever you feel the leash go tight, stop. Your dog will wonder why you are not moving and come to you. Reward your dog when it does and continue walking. After a few days, it will learn not to pull on the leash.

Separation Anxiety

Teach your pooch that you will always come back if it gets upset when you leave.

Make Coming and Going Low-Key

Don't make a big fuss about it by lavishing your dog with attention before you leave home and immediately after you walk in the door. Show your dog that you leaving and returning is not a big deal. Ignore your dog before leaving and for a couple of minutes when you return.

Teach Your Dog That You'll Return

Confine your dog to an area. Give it a chew toy and then leave your pooch for 5-10 minutes at first. Be calm when you go so that your dog knows its okay to be alone. When you step back, keep things quiet and give your dog time to relax. Once your dog is relaxed, step outside again.

Whining for Attention

Does your pooch whine to get your attention?

Ignore

If you look at the dog or pet it when it whines, you will teach your furry baby that whining works. Instead of giving it attention, turn your back when it whines. You can also leave the room or fold your arms and look away. Only play or pet your dog when it is not whining.

Barking at the Door

When someone is at the door, does your dog bark relentlessly?

Teach Your Dog a New Habit

Pick a spot or an area just within the sight of the door. Teach your dog to stay or lie down when you say "Go to your place." It will give your dog something else to do and be calm when someone is at the door. Ask a family or a friend to come to the door. When your dog remains calm and quiet, open the door and give it the treat as a reward. In this manner, it will learn to be calm and quiet to get the treat.

Jumping

Dogs naturally greet their human by jumping. But this can scare the guest away or can be dangerous for small children.

Don't Give It Attention

Pushing your dog away or yelling will only give your dog the attention it seeks. Ignore your dog when it starts to jump on you instead. Turn your back or cross your arm over your chest and don't make a sound. If your dog tries to run around to jump on you again, turn the other way around. You can also step outside of the door or room when your dog jumps on you when you walk in. Wait a few minutes and then step back. Repeat this method until your pooch is calm. It will help if you were to give it a treat for being calm.

Use the "Sit" Command

As soon as you are coming through the front door, tell your dog to "sit". Immediately reward with a treat. Repeat this method and your dog will be sitting as soon as you walk through the door or enter a room.

Biting

When a dog feels nervous or threatened, its natural tendency is to bite.

Socialize Your Dog Early

Introducing your dog to different people will make it more relaxed, especially with people with disabilities, children and the elderly. Exposing your dog to various situations such as loud noises, other animals, bicycles, large machines, cars and anything that might cause fear will lessen the anxiety to strange things and sounds.

Do Not Use Physical Punishment

Any violent punishment will make your pooch more aggressive or fearful. Always use positive reinforcement before resorting to hard training.

Warn Others

If your dog has aggressive or fearful tendencies, always warn other people and do not let your pooch approach other animals or people unless you are there to supervise and control.

Aggression

Any breed is capable of aggression. Behavioral problems such as snapping, growling or biting are scary and upsetting. You need to take steps to stop it.

Consult Your Veterinarian

Sudden signs of aggression may be due to some diseases or conditions that cause aggressive behavior in dogs. Talk to your pooch's Vet to determine if your dog needs medication or treatment to improve its behavior.

Contact a Professional Dog Trainer

If a medical problem is ruled out, do not try to fix your dog's aggression problem by yourself. This grave problem needs a behaviorist or trainer. A professional will create a plan for how to manage your dog's aggression.

Barking All the Time

Howling, barking and whining are dogs' ways to express themselves and communicate with humans. However, excessive barking is a problem.

Teach Your Dog Quiet Commands

This training must be done 1 to 2 times a day for 10 to 15 minutes each session.

1. Choose a quiet command, such as "quiet," "enough," or "hush".

2. When your dog barks, briefly acknowledge the source by going to your dog or looking out the door or window. Then, get its attention with a whistle, clap, or any similar sound.

3. Immediately, after your pooch stops barking, say your command in an audible, upbeat, and a firm voice while giving it a treat. Practice the command frequently, any time your dog barks, but keep the sessions brief.

Once your dog understands the quiet command, you can move to the voice command.

Teach Your Dog Voice Commands

1. Choose a bark command, such as "talk", "bark", or "speak".

2. Create a barking situation. The best method is to have a family member or a friend knock on the door or ring the doorbell. As your dog barks at the situation, say your command in an audible, upbeat, and firm voice.

3. After your pooch has barked 2 to 3 times in a row, say "good (talk, bark, or speech)" while giving it a treat.

4. Repeat the command process several times until your pooch understands.

Once your dog learns the "speak" and the "quiet" command separately, you can use them together – make your dog bark a few times, then tell it to be quiet.

Chapter 12 - Playtime & Games

Playing is a fundamental need, not only for dogs but also for humans. It is an incredible way to connect with our furry friends. Teaching your dog games is an excellent way to build your relationship. Playing with your dog builds confidence, trust and coping skills.

Benefits of Play

- Reinforcement for dogs who need to learn self-control
- Enriching – emotionally, physically and socially
- Reduces stress
- Enhances social skills
- Enhances training/learning
- Improves emotional state and welfare
- Promotes emotional resilience
- Healing
- Contagious
- Helps us geting to "know" our dogs
- Helps dogs make connections with people
- Healthy for them—and us
- FUN!

What Kind of Games Do Dogs Enjoy?

What's fun? Think like your dog. Think like a predator.

- Mind games
- Chasing games
- Running games

- Jumping games

- Hunting games (sniffing games)

Anything "fun" has playtime game potential!

However, while some dogs are comfortable to engage in play, other canine buddies are more challenging. Play preferences and styles greatly vary depending on your dog's genes, prior experiences, personality and emotional health.

To help you find the perfect game for your pooch, here are a few games that you can engage your dog in.

The "Chill Out" Game – The Calming Switch

This game is designed to use play as a reward for self-control. The method involves deliberately getting your dog excited to play and then having it "chill out" on command.

Here are the benefits of this game.

- Teaches dog instant calm from high arousal

- Installs an "on/off" switch

- Substitute calm behavior for agitated state

- Teaches dog calmness from high excitement situations

How to:

1. Teach your dog the command "sit" or "down". It is very crucial since this will be the base of this game.

2. Now get your pooch excited by playing chase or tugging a toy on a string, wrestling game or any game it regularly plays with you.

3. In the middle of the play, stop, be like a tree and command it to "sit" or lay "down."

4. Once your dog is calm, immediately reward it by starting the game again. Your dog will learn that the "sit" or "down" starts the game again.

5. Vary the length of the time your dog has to "sit" or stay "down" before playing again.

6. Change the command from "sit", "down" and "relax".

7. Vary the length of playing.

Toy Play

This fun way to connect and engage is the foundation for off lead control. The leash comes off! The toy comes out!

Fetch

1. Get two identical toys. Tennis balls, plush toys or whatever toy your dog likes to play with. The important thing is that the toys must be exactly the same. He needs to like both toys the same. If the toys are different, your dog might prefer the one over the other. When that happens, this technique will not work.

2. Offer one of the toys to your pooch and allow it to play with it. Don't take it away from your dog.

3. Now wave the other toy. Your pooch will likely drop the one he's playing with to grab the second one. Alternate the toys. Playfully tease your pooch to entice it.

4. Start tossing one of the toys a couple of feet at first. As soon as your dog goes and gets the thrown toy, call and encourage your dog to come back. You may have to run backward to encourage it to come to you.

5. When your pooch reaches you, show it the other toy that you are still holding. The dog will probably drop the toy it has to get the one you are holding. If not, you can trade the toy with a treat.

6. Throw the second toy. Your dog will run to get it. Start the process over again.

7. Start slow and build up the play over time. Always stop playing before your dog tires of the game.

Note: Toys designated for FETCH and TUG must be kept away when you are not playing games with your dog. It will help the toys stay fresh and enticing, leaving your pooch wanting more.

Tug

1. Encourage you pooch to grab a toy. Find a toy your dog likes by waving it in front of it. Reward it for getting the toy by letting your dog have it.

2. After a minute, get the toy back from your dog by "trading" for a tasty treat.

3. Wave the toy again.

4. Gradually work up to tugging. Some dogs are natural while others will need more encouragement.

5. Once the dog is "into" tugging games, it is time to begin teaching it some rules to play by:

   • Teach it to leave the toy on your cue or command.

   • Chose a release command, such as "mine" "leave it", "out" or "thank you".

- Once your dog releases it, give it a tasty reward. Next, cue your dog with commands, such as "tug", "get it" or "yours".
- Your furry buddy will learn to have the toy, release it, receive a reward for giving it and then to have it back again.
- The penalty for taking the toy when not invited is time-out or end of the game.
- If your dog nips your hand in the process, the game ends immediately.
- Your dog can get as excited as it wants as long as it plays by the rules. Your dog can growl, shake and tug all it wants.

6. Always stop the game before your dog tires of playing.

Chase It

You can purchase a chase and pull stick or a chase it squirrels from a pet store, or you can make your own using a dog toy and a horse lunge whip or a rope and a PVC pipe.

1. Using the pole, move the toy in erratic motions on the ground, combining with quick hop movements in the air.
2. Occasionally let your dog capture it.
3. Tell your dog to release the toy for a treat or toss the treat so the dog releases it.
4. Take breaks. Stop the toy movement.
5. Finally, the game ends when the squirrel dies.

Food Play

Most dogs love to play food games. These playtime activities are simple and only require food and a dog that is eager to eat.

Food Toss or Get It Game

The rule of this game is simple. You throw the food, and your pooch gets it. Repeat.

1. Begin with a short toss. Get the dog's attention by showing it the treat. Toss it. Be sure your dog sees where the food lands.

2. When your dog gets the first treat, wait until it returns or looks back at you. Toss another treat in the opposite direction.

Chase Me!

Dogs just love to run and chase. It's their natural way of playing with each other. Your four-legged buddy will consider it very cool that you know this game.

1. Stick to the rule. There is only one way to play this game. Your dog should chase you, not the other way around. Do not encourage your pooch to run away from you.

2. Run away from your dog and persuade it to run towards you by making some noise, giggle or clap. Running 5 to 10 feet away is enough.

3. When your dog is only a few feet away from you, toss a treat behind you so that it will keep running in your direction.

4. Then turn and run the other way.

5. Try incorporating obedience commands and chase games.

Note: End the game when the chase leads to over-exuberant jumping, mouthing or nipping. This game is not recommended for young kids for the reasons mentioned.

Catch

This trick is easy to teach using big, light, fluffy and easy to catch popcorn. You can use any food for this game.

1. Buy a bag of popcorn and toss one at the time.

2. Be patient. Co-ordination may take time, but your dogs motor skills will slowly develop.

See It, Drop It

This game uses food to teach your pooch impulse control as it learns to wait and look at the food before being cued to "Get it."

1. Gently restrain your dog so that it will wait to see the treat.

2. The game will progress until your pooch waits and sees it on its own.

3. Drop the treat. Gently restrain your dog when it tries to get it. When your dog is settled, say "Get it," removing the restraint and allowing it to get the food.

4. The dog will eventually learn to see it, wait and on cue get it, if you drop or toss a treat.

Target Game (Nose-first) with Food

The easiest way to start this game is by teaching your dog to touch its nose to a target held close to its nose. You can use a pencil, a sticky note or your hand for smaller dogs and a tennis ball for larger dogs.

1. Choose an appropriate target for your pooch.

2. Show it with the target. Present it swiftly to your dog, about a quarter of an inch in front of its nose. Give your dog a treat as soon as it looks at the target.

3. If your dog touches it the right way, then reward it.

4. Again, show your dog the target at a quarter inch from its nose. As soon as your dog touches it with its nose, reward it.

5. Once your pooch learns, you can move the target a little to the right or left, a little lower or higher. Reward your dog once it touches the target with its nose.

6. Play no more than 3 to 5 minutes at a time.

Place

This play is a type of target game, wherein your dog's bed, a platform or a mat is the target place. The aim of this game is to make your pet go to a place and when your dog does, it earns a reward.

1. Begin with no more than a foot away from the place.

2. Refrain from luring your dog into the area. Instead, get it to do it by itself and then reward your dog after.

3. Show your dog the treat and then use your body language, such as leaning or looking towards the place.

4. Reward your dog immediately with every successful contact with its place. You can give your dog the treat with your hands or toss the treats and say "get it" as a food toss game.

5. After your dog readily goes to its place, begin to add the command "place."

6. Once your dog learns, move a little farther away. Stay at this distance and stare at it until your dog goes to its place by itself. The moment your dog sets foot on the place, toss a reward.

7. Gradually increase the distance.

If your pooch is not familiar with a mat or a platform, then introduce it first. Encourage your dog to walk over it, sniff it or give it a few treats on the place before you begin the game.

Leave It!

This game teaches the dog to leave the treat, not grab it from your hand, and then take treats from your hand gently. You can readily show this to your dog as it wants the food you are holding.

1. Hold a tasty treat in your hand.

2. Close your hand to form a fist to hide the treat inside and hold it to your dog. It will likely sniff, try to nibble, paw and lick.

3. Quietly wait until your dog stops investigating your fist and moves its nose away. The moment it does, say "Yes" and then open your hand, allowing it to eat the treat from your flat open palm.

4. When your dog learns to refrain from getting the treat, you can say, "Leave it."

5. When your dog is doing well, try offering the treat with an open hand. The goal is to make your dog "leave it" until you

give it permission to do so. Quickly close your hand when it tries.

6. When your dog learns well, you can try different situations, such as a treat on the ground, a chair, etc.

7. Remember to add the cue "leave it" when your dog is reliably refraining from taking the treat. Also, use the signal "TREAT" to let your dog know that it has permission to take it.

Physical Play

When your dog shows little interest in toys and food games, playing physical games will light the mood up and make it come alive.

Hide and Seek

1. Quickly leave the room and then hide. Call out to your pet and wait.

2. Hopefully, your dog will search to find you. When it does, you can tease it by hiding your face or giggling. You also can pet your dog when it finds you.

Touch

1. Hold your palm near your pooch's face and wait until it touches it with its nose. Reward your dog with a treat. When your dog mouths your hand, do not reward it. Only a nose touch is allowed.

2. As your pet learns to touch your palm with its nose, gradually put your hand in other positions so that your dog will have to move to reach it.

Touch is the foundation of lift and spin.

Lift

1. Hold your hand above your dog's head in a manner that it has to lift up to touch it.

2. You can slowly progress to make your dog do an impressive leap to touch your hand, which is fun for many dogs.

Spin

1. Move your hand following a small clockwise circle over your dog's nose. As your pet follows your hand, it will turn in a tight circle.

2. Slowly fade your hand as your dog learns to spin until it does it only with a hand gesture as the cue.

Go Wild and Freeze

1. Look at your pooch and say "Go wild", and then get excited, get silly, jump around and make some noise. It will encourage your dog to be playful as well.

2. After a moment, say "Freeze," then turn away from it, cross your arms and be quiet.

3. When your pet is calm, "go wild" and then freeze again.

Chapter 13 - Easy Cool Tricks

When you are training your dog, it is easy to focus on good manners and obedience. However, breaking free from the routine and teaching your buddy new tricks will give your dog a chance to take a break and have fun. At the same time, tricks build better communication and strengthen your relationship, which augments your obedience training.

General Trick Training Tips

- Make sure that your pooch is giving 100 percent of its attention before you start teaching it any tricks.

- Use small, bite-sized pieces of treats as rewards. Prepare them before so that you can immediately reward your dog for good behavior.

- Give your dog lots of praise.

- Stay positive – training should be fun for your dog and you.

- Keep sessions short -15 minutes maximum is ideal.

- Be patient –some dogs learn faster than others do.

- If your dog is not in the mood, then do something else.

- Speak consistently and firmly, never with frustration or anger.

- Always end each session on a positive note. When your dog performs a trick successfully, reward and praise it for a good job.

Crawl

When your dog has mastered the "lie down" command, teach it this next trick.

1. Make your dog lie down.

2. Kneel next to your dog with a treat

3. Hold the treat in your hand just in front of its nose. Get your dog to lean towards it.

4. If your dog is getting up, use your free hand to gently keep its body in a crawling position.

5. Gradually move the treat away from your dog so that it has to lean forward to sniff the treat. When your dog starts to crawl forward on its tummy after the treat, say the command "crawl."

6. Repeat until your dog learns the idea of crawling on its belly without a treat in your hand.

7. After that, place the treat a few feet in front of your pooch's nose and then drag your finger along the floor towards it, while saying the command "crawl."

8. Finally, practice without tracing your fingers on the floor, getting your dog to crawl to the treat with only the verbal cue.

Shake Hands

This classic trick is an all-time favorite.

1. Sit facing your dog.

2. Rest your hand next to one of its shoulders. Gently press so that it can keep balance when you raise your dogs paw.

3. Take its front leg with your other hand say "shake hands."

4. Reward your dog with a treat.

5. Repeat until your dog raises its paw perfectly on cue.

Tail Chase

Dogs often chase their tails. But can you get your dog to chase its tail on your command?

1. Hold the treat in front of your dog's nose.

2. Slowly move the treat around your dog's body at tail height.

3. As your pet chases the treat say, "chase tail."

4. Reward your dog with the treat. Repeat.

5. Practice the trick using the same gesture but without the treat.

6. Then practice the method just by saying the command, "chase tail."

7. When your dog masters the trick, always reward and praise it.

Speak

Sometimes, dog's think that they are human. Well, what else can you do about it? Teach your dog how to speak, of course.

1. Command your dog to sit.

2. Hold the treat just of your dog's sniffing range. This will excite and tempt it.

3. Now move your hand, the one holding the treat, to your back, hiding it from your dog and wait for it to bark.

4. Just before it barks, say, "speak." Praise your dog when it barks and reward with the treat.

5. Repeat the process. Eventually, as your dog learns the trick, you won't have to hide the treat. You will only need to say, "Speak." and your dog will bark on command.

Note: You can use a gesture along with your verbal command. Try opening your hand into a quacking motion when you say, "speak". Soon, the hand gesture will be enough to tell your dog to speak.

Roll Over

Your dog will love this trick.

1. Get your buddy to "drop" and lie down on its side.
2. Hold the treat near the side of its mouth.
3. As your dog turns its head towards it, move the treat further away from your dog so that it will complete a roll over on its back.
4. When your dog completes a roll, praise and reward with the treat.

Beg

What could be cuter than a dog sitting on its hind legs with the front paws up?

1. Command your dog in the stay or sit position.
2. Hold the treat just above its nose so that it has to look up to the treat.
3. As your dog reaches with its mouth, raise the treat higher until your dog is sitting on its hind legs with its front paws off the ground.
4. Reinforce this action by saying the command "beg." Quickly reward your dog with the treat.

5. Repeat until your dog masters the trick.

Note: If your pooch jumps before begging, pull the treat away and say "no." Reset with stay or sit. Try again.

Wacky Walk

This impressive trick involves your four-legged friend to weave in and out of your legs as you walk. It may take some time to learn so be patient.

1. Start with your buddy sitting or standing on your left side.

2. With your right foot, take a step forward. Hold the treat behind your right leg and encourage your pooch to move between your legs. Praise it and reward with the treat.

3. Once your buddy gets comfortable walking between your legs in one direction, say the command "wacky walk." as your dog does.

4. As your pooch moves between your legs, offer another treat to make it walk in front of your body.

5. With your left foot, step in an exaggerated walk and say "wacky walk."

6. Encourage your dog to walk between your legs the other way.

7. Continue to reward with a treat until your dog learns the "wacky walk."

Cross the Road

Dogs lack common sense when it comes to crossing a road. Here's a trick that will teach your dog how to cross the road safely.

1. Put your dog on a collar and leash. Walk it to the edge of the footpath, facing the traffic.
2. If your dog barks at cars or pulls away, tug it back and reprimand it.
3. Before you cross the road, command it to "sit."
4. Pause until the road is clear.
5. Say the command "walk" and cross the road.
6. If your dog crosses the road ahead of you, pull it back to your side saying "heel."
7. When your dog crosses the road correctly, praise and reward it with a treat.

Jump

Dogs just love to jump. It's in their nature. Harness that love for jumping into a trick.

1. Put your dog on a collar and leash.
2. Find a log or a low wall for your pooch to jump over.
3. Command it to sit.
4. Step over to the other side and say "over".
5. Gently tug on the leash.
6. Reward your dog when it gets over the obstacle.
7. Repeat until your dog learn the trick with a command only and without you to lead.
8. Praise and reward as your dog master the trick.

Conclusion

Thank you for buying this book on Dog Training by Catherine Lewis!

I hope this book was able to help you and your dog's transition into your new life together and make your new journey a fun and easy adventure. A life with a dog is rewarding and more meaningful, especially when you know how to properly raise and train your pooch.

The next step is to follow the tips and advice in this book. Don't forget to follow your heart as well. With your knowledge and your heart to guide, you can never be wrong.

You find more in-depth Dog Training by visiting
www.tiny.cc/dogcoaching

And if you wish to learn how to make your own, healthy dog food, please visit **www.tiny.cc/healthydogfood**

Notes

Here you can keep notes to measure your progress. Remember to add dates.

_____

_____

_____

_____

_____

_____

_____

_____

_____

_____

_____

_____

_____

_____

_____

_____

_____

_____

Notes

Notes

Notes

Notes

Notes

Notes

Notes

Notes

Printed in Great Britain
by Amazon